Edinburgh

Steps into History

ELSPETH WILLS & JENNIE RENTON

**Main Point
BOOKS**

First published 2024
ISBN 978-1-7395214-3-1

The authors' right to be identified as authors of this book
under the Copyright, Designs and Patents Act 1988 has been asserted

This book is printed on FSC-certified paper in a printing house that uses
100% renewably-sourced energy

Printed and bound by
Totem Printing House

Typeset in Minion Pro and Blackbeard by
Main Point Books, Edinburgh

Cover image: bard and herbalist Lewis Cowan at the top of the Vennel Steps
Photograph by Jennie Renton

Text © Jennie Renton and Elspeth Wills
Map © Roger Emmerson
Photographs © Jennie Renton unless otherwise stated

Contents

Map of Places of Interest on the Vennel	5
Introduction	9
Now and Then in the Grassmarket	13
West Port Community Garden	18
Portsburgh Chapel & the Salvation Army Hostel	24
Brown's Place, off the Vennel	30
State of the Vennel	34
Synagogue Back Door	36
The Suffragette Piper Girl, Bessie Watson	39
The Child Garden	42
The Flodden & Telfer Walls	47
Burke, Hare & the Vennel Alibi	53
Heriot's and its Founder, Jinglin Geordie	58
Playing with Fire at All Hallows Fair	62
The Vennel in Film and TV	64

Memories & Trivia	66
Image credits	69
About the Contributors	71
Local Organisations	72

The Vennel Steps, mapped by Roger Emmerson.

Vennel:

A narrow alley or lane between houses, still frequent in many street names in Scotland.

(Scottish National Dictionary)

Introduction

As a visitor to Edinburgh, the Vennel Steps will be on your must-visit list as the best spot to picture yourself (and friends and lovers) against the backdrop of the Castle. If you are local, the Vennel is perhaps no more than a handy shortcut when escaping the hubub of the Grassmarket for the green expanse of the Meadows.

You may not realise that the Vennel has a rich and tantalisingly hidden history – its many stories have been overshadowed by the Grassmarket's more lurid tales of public executions and riots. We decided that the Vennel deserves a guide book of its own. And here it is!

Hurtling fireballs and false alibis. A garden created for and worked by slum children. A hostel for homeless women. The chapel where 'Lifters' and 'Anti-Lifters' fell out. The birthplace of Scotland's youngest (bagpiper) Suffragette. Walls built to protect the city from English invasion. These are all part of the Vennel story. Come with us back in time and step into the Vennel's history.

Elspeth Wills and Jennie Renton,
August 2024

Now and Then in the Grassmarket

Throngs of visitors create a phenomenal buzz in this history-drenched rectangle at the foot of the castle rock. Independent shops and weekend open-air markets offer the quirky, the curated and the artisanal in food and fashion. This is the only place in Edinburgh where, within 200 metres end to end, you can buy a handmade hat, a designer knit and a cashmere scarf; drink in a pub where Rabbie Burns once enjoyed a nip and a chaser; potter along to Victoria Street, the original Diagon Alley; or join the queue up the Vennel Steps looking forward to a Mary's Milk Bar gelato, freshly made that morning.

The crowds in the Grassmarket get more intense with every year that passes and this does bring some problems for residents, whose community association, GRASS, campaigns for a sustainable balance between community and tourism.

Passionate about their home territory, local activists try to get the word out that the Grassmarket is not just a hollow, scenic venue something akin to a stage set – real people actually live there.

Archaeological excavations made in 2006 revealed traces of two Bronze Age fire pits, indicating that there has been human activity in the area for at least 5,000 years. But the first written record naming the Grassmarket is in a charter issued in 1477 by King James III, granting its right to operate as a market.

The photograph opposite, taken by George Washington Wilson around the 1860s, shows heavily loaded, horse-drawn carts on the cobbles. The Black Bull Inn, the Carriers' Warehouse and a tobacco and snuff merchant can be seen clearly. Sadly, because they were in motion, most of the people are little more than a ghost-like blur.

Victorian detective James McLevy described the Grassmarket as a bustling hubbub full of street stalls:

> Some are enveloped in a mountain of shining articles of tin, others by a forest of wicker work others in a heap of black tin shovels. Many are devoted to kitchens where they show their white caps to the servants out of a basket. Apple and orange sellers are everywhere.

By the mid-19th century when McLevy was writing, the West Port had degenerated into a slum. Contemporary artists' impressions and engravings

THE CASTLE, FROM THE VENNEL, EDINBURGH.

of the Grassmarket and environs, such as Shepherd's Edinburgh Castle viewed from the Vennel and Channing's drawing of Ballantyne's Close, present the scene as romantic, unpolluted and orderly. Airbrushed out was the chronic filth and overcrowding that prevailed: forty or more families might occupy a single tenement stair. Travellers often mentioned the stench from sewage waste tossed out of windows with the warning cry of 'gardyloo'... if you were lucky.

BALLANTYNE'S CLOSE, GRASSMARKET, 1850. (*From a Drawing by W. Channing.*)

West Port Community Garden

The beautiful garden full of mature trees that rises steeply from the West Port parallel with the Vennel, came into community hands eleven years ago, in partnership with Edinburgh Council. It was designed by one of Scotland's first female landscape architects, Norah Geddes (1887–1967). She was involved in the creation of community gardens in Edinburgh's Old Town, at Chessel's Court and Johnston Terrace. Embodying the principles of outdoor learning promoted by the free kindergarten movement which was strongly active in Edinburgh, the aim was to enable children living in dark, overcrowded tenements to experience nature through growing flowers and vegetables and other creative outdoor activities.

By 1910 Norah was making her mark as a member of the Open Spaces Committee founded by her father, pioneer ecologist and town planner Patrick Geddes. The Geddes family lived at Ramsay Garden, just off the Lawnmarket near Edinburgh Castle esplanade.

An inspiring social activist and innovator, Patrick had set up the 'Open Spaces Committee' to highlight the impact of poor housing and poverty on public health

and wellbeing. Pragmatic as well as visionary, Patrick's interventions pointed the way to an approach to town planning that was both enlightened and possible. Responding to an initiative from the Edinburgh Social Union, the local council was persuaded to lease several pockets of land where green spaces could be created – 'green lungs' for the city.

One of the sites chosen was a steep strip of derelict land at the foot of the West Port, near the entrance to the Vennel. A surviving delicate watercolour sketch by Norah, which looks to have been a 'mirror-image' of her design for West Port, shows her plan for the slopes by the King's Wall, below the Castle: planting areas laid out in terraces, intersected with paths and stairs.

West Port Garden was opened in 1906 and for some years Norah acted as its superintendent. It was home to a scout company and a boxing club, as well as ongoing gardening activities.

The end of the Second World War saw the winding up of the Open Spaces Committee. West Port Garden was handed back to Edinburgh Corporation and for decades it was locked up, choked with weeds.
In 2014 the local community association, GRASS,

established a group of volunteer gardeners to look after West Port Garden. Immense amounts of planting and conservation work were done over the next decade.

At the top of the slope a row of planters have been installed for growing vegetables and herbs. A stunning view of Edinburgh Castle is available from this unique vantage point. The picture opposite, taken in summertime, shows the castle rising above a dense tree canopy. The view changes dramatically through the seasons: as the trees shed their leaves in autumn and through the winter months, the castle rock becomes fully revealed. Then is spring, the castle is once more framed in fresh greenery.

In 2024 GRASS marked the tenth anniversary of their custody of the Garden with the unveiling of a banner (pictured on page 18), gifted by stitchers from neighbouring Lister Housing Cooperative and dedicated to 'Norah Geddes, Pioneer Gardener'.

Ground level access to West Port Garden has recently been improved and a seating area and sensory garden created behind the police box. The Garden is often open, but most regularly on dry Sunday afternoons, 2–4pm.

Portsburgh Chapel & the Salvation Army Hostel

The former Portsburgh Chapel was originally founded in the late 18th century by the 'Anti-Burghers', a breakaway movement from the Secession Church, which was itself a breakaway from the Church of Scotland.

The Anti-Burghers then went on to split into virulently opposing factions over what came to be known as the 'Lifter' controversy – whether the minister should or should not lift the bread during the sacrament. Disparaging epithets were lobbed back and forth with incendiary energy. *Absurd confusions! Unfair representations! Sophistical impositions!*

Plain daft! might have been the view of their Old Town neighbours, so many of whom were struggling to put bread on the table to feed their families.

The present building dates from 1828 and is B-listed. Recognisable by its arcaded porch, it stands halfway up the Vennel. It is the oldest surviving building on the steps.

In 1881 the chapel was taken over by the Salvation Army, which was expanding its operation into Scotland; the Portsburgh Chapel was their first base in Edinburgh. This 'Army' of 'Christian soldiers' sought to convert poor people and save them from the ravages of the 'demon drink'. As a first salvo, their Chief of Staff, Colonel Edmonds, organised an 'Exhibition of Drunkards' at the George Street Music Hall, entitled 'Trophies of the Army's Work in Glasgow'. But the event was infiltrated by rowdies and Salvation Army personnel were reportedly mobbed, crushed and ill-treated:

> Interruptions and cat-calls made speeches almost impossible. The furniture of the Music Hall was badly damaged and the bandsmen had to return home without their instruments for fear of their being destroyed by roughs on the way to the station.

Edmonds' hope was to transform folk 'dug out of the black holes of the Grassmarket and neighbourhood', into a congregation with 'bright, shining faces' and 'nicely combed heads of hair'. However, the Salvation Army top brass did not share his optimism that this could be achieved from premises situated 'in a back street, amidst an Irish mob, in a proud, dead and half-damned city', as scathingly put by W. Bramwell

Booth, son of the Salvation Army's founder. In 1884 the Salvation Army converted Portsburgh Chapel into a shelter capable of accommodating up to a hundred women at very modest rates. It was full from the first month of opening, reflecting the demand in the community.

In 1912 the accommodation was expanded, providing cheap accommodation for 'RESPECTABLE WOMEN needing a safe and comfortable home'. The new premises, a handsome building faced in red sandstone, still stands at the corner of the Vennel at the foot of the West Port; it is connected by corridors to the old chapel building.

In Victorian and Edwardian times, women residents could often be seen sitting on the Vennel Steps puffing away on their clay pipes, the acrid odour of tobacco mingling with the smell of home-made soup drifting up from the basement kitchen of the hostel.

Today, the whole complex is the Kick Ass backpackers' hostel, catering for visitors to Edinburgh's Old Town, many of whom are keen to be pictured on the adjacent Vennel Steps. The beautifully carved art nouveau lettering above the hostel doorway is a reminder of its days as a place of refuge for women who had fallen on hard times.

Brown's Place, off the Vennel

Brown's Place is an attractive square opening onto the Vennel, situated about halfway up the steps. It was built by James Brown (not to be confused with an earlier architect also called James Brown, who designed the once famously beautiful George Square, now despoiled by University of Edinburgh development).

Our James Brown ran a stables in the Grassmarket, where he also owned an inn close to the entrance to the Vennel. The building on the north side of Brown's Place, intended as his family home, is now divided into five flats. It is likely Brown used rubble from the demolished sections of the Flodden Wall for his buildings. The residents have created a shared garden and drying green where there was once a concrete desert.

Brown's Place Residents Association website tells us:

> In 1834 Brown's Place, described as 'newly built' was advertised for sale along with the inn. It was again advertised in 1853 and continued to be sold as a unit at least until 1947.

State of the Vennel

From *The Scotsman*, 1867 (it took over a century before the writer's comments were addressed):

> For years farmers have been complaining of the dangerous state of the Vennel – the great thoroughfare on Wednesdays between the corn and the cattle markets. Every market-day, limb and life are endangered here; and scarcely a Wednesday passes without some one falling and injuring himself. On Wednesday last there were two or three tumbles, and it is not at all improbable that some day we shall have to report a case of a fatal accident here – entirely owing to the unsafe character of the passage; in which case the Streets and Buildings or Paving Board authorities, who have often been warned about the disgraceful condition of the Vennel, could hardly be held altogether blameless. If the nature of the ground precludes them from making the road less steep, they should at least break the steepness by a flight of steps, such as we see in other parts of the city, and place a railing along the side. This would cause no great expense, and it is the more called for that those whose lives are weekly imperilled contribute no inconsiderable proportion to the city revenues.

Synagogue Back Door

Just beyond the arches of the Portsburgh Chapel are the gates to the back entrance of the Graham Street Synagogue, which occupied the former Greyfriars Free Church from 1892 to 1932. The rabbi's son David Daiches wrote about the synagogue in his memoir *Two Worlds*, saying 'the approach from the east was by a picturesque narrow lane called the Vennel'. He writes:

> On a clear day the dusk would turn true violet in colour, and the dark outline of the Castle would stand out in the horizon in romantic gloom. (Many years later they took to floodlighting it, which was picturesque but not the same thing: the gas light in the windows of the little shops in the back streets, with their tinsel decorations and cheap Christmas goods, was the most moving illumination I ever saw in Edinburgh.)

The gates now lead to Edinburgh College of Art, which occupies the land where the cattle market once stood. Within the gates can be seen flax plants, grown so that students in the Textiles Department can experiment with extracting natural dyes.

The Suffragette Piper Girl: Bessie Watson, 11 the Vennel

Bessie Watson, Scotland's, and possibly Britain's youngest suffragette, was born at 11 Vennel in 1900, 'in the very shadow of the castle', as she recalls in her memoir, *Lone Piper*. Her house and its neighbours have now vanished and 6VT Youth Cafe stands in their place.

Housing conditions in Edinburgh's Old Town were damp, unhealthy and overcrowded. Tuberculosis – the 'White Plague' – was rife. By the age of seven, Bessie had already lost a brother and an aunt to the disease. She was sent to bagpipe lessons on the advice of the family doctor, as a way of strengthening her lungs.

'Hen-toed and bandy-legged', as she later described herself, Bessie was too small to manage even the smallest set of pipes. A 'baby' chanter – the pipe with finger holes on which the melody is played – was ordered from a bagpipe maker at the top of the Mound.

Bessie was lucky to be taught by a Pipe Major who soon realised that his young pupil was a natural and did everything to encourage her. She loved the instrument and swiftly moved on to the full set of bagpipes.

When Bessie was nine, her toddler brother died suddenly of TB, leaving her 'lost and lonely'. Shortly after this tragic loss, the family happened to be taking a walk along Queensferry Street, off the west end of Princes Street. Drawn to a window dressed in the colours of the suffragette movement – purple, white and green – Bessie and her mother went inside to find out more about the Women's Social and Political Union (WSPU).

This chance event won Bessie Watson her place in suffragette history. The following Saturday, as a new member of the WSPU, Bessie was one of the youngest people to take part in a huge march and pageant demanding Votes for Women – she was certainly the youngest piper.

The brooch presented to Bessie Watson by the WSPU. In her old age she gifted it to Margaret Thatcher, the first female Prime Minister in the UK.

Bessie Watson taking part in a suffragette march, aged around 11.

Bessie was dedicated to the campaign for women's right to vote. When fellow suffragettes were imprisoned in Edinburgh's Calton Gaol she would sometimes play her pipes outside the building to raise their spirits, especially those on hunger strike who were being force-fed. She did the same in Waverley Station when suffragettes were being put on trains to be transported to London to serve their sentences in Holloway Prison.

The Child Garden

A tragic but ultimately heart-warming story lies behind the creation of the 'child garden' at the top of the Vennel Steps (now 6VT Youth Café).

At the outbreak of the First World War, James Hamilton Maxwell from Edinburgh was a student at the University of Oxford, where he played cricket for the Wadham College team. He served in the trenches and was wounded, but shortly after his return to the front at Ypres he lost his life, aged 22. From his teenage years, James had been a keen outdoors person who loved nothing better than to set off on his bicycle with a home-made tent in search of wilderness. His camping expeditions took him to the Highlands of Scotland, particularly the Cairngorms.

In 1925, ten years after his death, his parents bought the land where 11–15 Vennel once stood. They established a child garden there, dedicated to the memory of their son, for the benefit of local slum children, giving them a chance to enjoy fresh air and outdoor play. But after James's parents passed away, the trust lapsed and the child garden was taken over

The Vennel in 1900. The Child Garden was founded on the site of the houses on the left.

by the city council and turned into the Grassmarket Nursery with places for 24 pre-school children.

By 2013 numbers attending the nursery had plummeted and the decision was made to relocate it to nearby Tollcross Primary School. Today, the ethos of the original child garden finds fresh expression in 6VT Youth Café, the current tenants of the child garden premises whose mission is:

to provide a quality, safe environment for young people to come together to access a range of services and personal development opportunities which motivate and inspire them to improve their lives and of those around them and to develop to the best of their potential.

Looking to the future, hopefully this special place on the Vennel continues to be dedicated to improving life for young people, in keeping with the wishes of James's parents, and will not fall prey to the office, hotel and student flat development that afflicts the city centre.

On the site of 6VT Café once stood the childhood home of Bessie Watson.

The Flodden & Telfer Walls

After the defeat of the Scots and the death of King James IV at the Battle of Flodden in 1513, the Flodden Wall was built in panic that England were about to invade – an invasion that never came. However, it served as a way of controlling the plague and keeping out smugglers.

The wall, around 1.2 metres thick and as high as 7.3 metres, ran from the south side of the castle, across the Grassmarket and up the Vennel. The couple pictured on the facing page are looking towards the only surviving bastion of the city wall: the remains of this watch-tower stand at the head of the Vennel.

Embrasures in the stone indicate defensive positions for soldiers to stave off attackers with arrows or, later, guns. When you look through the hole closest to the top of the steps, you are rewarded with an intriguingly framed view of the castle. There is also a blocked up window created in the 19th century.

The Telfer Wall, an extension to the Flodden Wall constructed in the early 1600s, takes its name from its builder, master mason John Taillefer (see picture on facing page). It is noticeable that the stones used to build the Flodden Wall are smaller than those in the Telfer Wall. Allegedly this is because women and children played a large part in its construction, due to the loss of so many young male Scots in the battle, but more than likely it was just because this was what was available.

John Taillefer sold a plot of land to George Heriot – Jinglin' Geordie, as he was nicknamed –who had amassed a fortune as moneylender to King James VI and I. Heriot used some of his fortune to found a school for the orphaned sons of merchants.

Both walls were gradually demolished in the 18th and 19th centuries. In 1829 there was a move to demolish the tower, because it was as 'a lurking place' for thieves. Fortunately, it survived. Rubble from parts of the wall that were demolished may have been used in building the houses in Brown's Place.

The picture opposite, taken just beyond the point where the Telfer Wall continues the Flodden Wall, shows it running along Heriot Place towards Lauriston Place as part of the George Heriot's School boundary. Until 1856, following the route of the walls, the Vennel was an official boundary of the city of Edinburgh.

Left: A toddler explores a gunloop slot, with trefoiled loops at top and bottom, in the Flodden Wall tower at the top of the Vennel. Above: In 1876 Edinburgh Council breached the wall to construct a window, according to the gilded inscription which recounts this dubious planning decision. It was later bricked up.

William Burke as he appeared at the bar. From a drawing made in court by George Lutenor.

Burke, Hare & the Vennel Alibi

Murderers Burke and Hare are two of Edinburgh's most notorious characters. In the 1820s, the city was a world-renowned centre of medical learning and research. The university Anatomy Department was headed by Dr Robert Knox, whose cadaver dissections were as popular as theatrical performances. It seems the chronic shortage of dead bodies caused Knox to fall into the habit of purchasing them without probing too deeply as to how they had been procured. William Burke, a regular supplier, was paid around £7 10s for each corpse. If Knox realised he was sourcing the bodies through murder, this has never been proved.

At least 16 people were murdered by Burke and his accomplice, William Hare. Their usual *modus operandi* was to lure some vulnerable person back to Burke's home in Tanner's Close, off the north side of the West Port, then ply the victim with drink until they passed out, or became incapable, and then suffocate them.

The 'Vennel alibi' emerged at the trial of William Burke and his common-law wife, Helen McDougal. To save his skin, Hare had turned King's evidence and testified

Helen McDougal being chased by an Edinburgh mob after her trial for murder.

against the couple, who were charged with several counts of murder. Accused of being party to the killing of a woman called Madge, McDougal admitted that the old lady had indeed visited them, but had got roaring drunk and left for home. She testified that she knew Madge was still alive the following night, as she had seen her in the Vennel, and Madge had apologised for her behaviour.

McDougal's defence lawyer, Lord Cockburn, stated:

> I have no doubt whatever, that the whole of these statements are false. I admit that they were mere inventions, fallen upon to conceal the crime. But this is not only their explanation, but their defence. She [McDougal] was aware of the suspected, or the guilty, trade which her husband was engaged in; and I have not a doubt that she was obliged to resort to similar deceptions every week. It was her misfortune to live in a situation in which, even when there was no idea of anything like murder, she was habitually obliged to make false statements to account for the possession of dead bodies, or to avoid the suspicion of having them.

The verdict on McDougal was 'not proven', but Burke was found guilty. He was hanged in public in 1829. The ambitious Dr Knox fell from grace, his career ruined.

The Crime of Miss Jean Brodie

As part of the centenary celebrations for Muriel Spark in 2018, Edinburgh Council put up heritage signs for 'The Miss Jean Brodie Steps' at the top and bottom of the Vennel. In the 1969 film *The Prime of Miss Jean Brodie*, the narcissistic but charismatic history teacher, played by Maggie Smith, is shown leading a group of James Gillespie's schoolgirls down the Vennel to the Grassmarket – a scene that does not occur in the novel.

The heritage signs were controversial. Welcomed by some as an appropriate homage to a brilliant author, others perceived an underhand attempt to rename the Vennel. Soon after they appeared, person or persons unknown took matters into their own hands and removed the signs under cover of darkness.

Muriel Spark was a meticulous and subtle stylist who planned every detail of her books before setting pen to paper. In choosing the name 'Brodie', she obliquely references the dualism of the city, embodied in the 18th century burglar Deacon Brodie, respectable cabinet-maker by day, devious criminal and gambler by night – to whom Miss Jean Brodie claims kinship in the novel.

Deacon Brodie (right) with George Smith, one of his accomplices, pictured by John Kay.

Heriot's and its Founder, Jinglin Geordie

George Heriot – goldsmith, moneylender and jeweller to King James VI – left a bequest of £23,625 'for the education, nursing and upbringing of youth, being puir orphans and fatherless children of decayet burgesses and freemen of the said burgh destitute, and left without means'.

Building started four years after Jinglin Geordie's death in 1624 and went on for decades. Replete with gargoyles and ornate chimneys, domes and turrets, gothic windows and multiple sundials carved in stone, the former Heriot's Hospital is now George Heriot's fee-paying school (girls were first admitted as pupils in the 1970s). It is one of the most magnificent buildings in Edinburgh. The picture opposite shows the southwest tower.

After the Battle of Dunbar in 1650 it was requisitioned by Oliver Cromwell for use as a military hospital. When it was restored to its original purpose in 1659, the first intake was 30 pupils; by the end of the 18th century there were 140 Heriot's boys. Numerals hewn into the flagstones in the inner courtyard indicate where pupils used to assemble each morning for register to be taken.

Detail from a John Slezer print of Heriot's Hospital showing the original cupolas on the southern towers, which were removed in the late 17th century. The building is surrounded by the extended Flodden Wall.

An incident in the 17th century involving boys from Heriot's Hospital shows how word-of-mouth could match today's social media as a toxic vector of mis/information.

In 1681 the Scottish Test Act was introduced, with the aim of preventing Catholics from taking positions of power. Despite having been active in suppressing Catholic highland chiefs, Archibald Campbell, 9th Earl of Argyll, questioned the wording of the Test Act and was tried for treason. This sparked outrage, with another nobleman protesting that even the English would not 'hang a dog' on such a trumped-up charge. Perhaps this got to the ears of certain Heriot's boys, who decided that the dog which guarded the school yard was in a position of public responsibility and must take the Test. The dog showed no interest in the printed Test Act thrust under his nose, and as Lauder of Fountainhall reported in his contemporary journal,

> loving a bone rather than it, [the dog] absolutely refused it. Then they rubbed it all over with butter… and he licked off the butter and did spit out the paper.

At this failure to comply with the Test, the boys decided to conduct their own trial by jury, found the animal guilty of treason, and actually hanged the poor creature.

Playing with Fire at All Hallows Fair

The Hallows Fair in the Grassmarket traditionally took place at the start of November, shortly after Hallowe'en. In the 18th century, a time when Health & Safety regulations were a figment of the future, the climax of the proceedings was a fiery game of football played in and all around the Grassmarket. This is graphically described in Alison Dunlop's *Anent Old Edinburgh* (1888):

> The principal event, the crowning *feu-de-joie* of the evening, was the rival turpentine balls. These balls were larger than a modern football. They were constructed of wire filled with tow and rags which had been fed, and gorged, and steeped with oil and turpentine for days beforehand. In fact, the morality of a turpentine ball was the very antithesis of modern teetotalism; its excellence was determined by its powers of suction. The balls had long wire strings, and were the work and care of all the apprentices of their respective districts.

> The Grassmarket ball came out of the 'Roperie' of Samuel Gilmore, after whom Gilmore Place is named; and the West Port ball from 'Yeben Gairdner's', the yarn-boiler in the Vennel. Set on fire, the balls were whirled

round, sling fashion, and swung off high and far into the air. They simply fell where they landed. Then ensued a game with no rules – Rugby, Association or otherwise – a fiery football. The danger was minimised in the broad platz of the Grassmarket, but in crowded Portsburgh the wonder is that there was not an annual conflagration. The hottest of the fray was on the site of the old city gate. The Vennel was created for a surprise party, and the Ferry Road, now the Low Castle Road, for an ambush.

The aim on one side was to capture the Edinburgh ball, on the other to kick the Portsburgh ball up the Grassmarket. In spite of burns and bruises and broken heads, these balls were as keenly fought for, taken, and gallantly regained as were ever regimental colours upon the battlefield. The last spark of the latest bonfire at length died out, the sorely distraught rulers of city and burgh, once more through their annual torture, could lay their heads on a well-earned pillow, and peace and order returned with the morning.

Dunlop also informs us that 'Tricorne firecrackers were once popular, and in the 18th century, the boys of Heriot's Hospital excelled in the manufacture of a famed species of three-cornered cocked-hat cracker.'

The Vennel in Film & TV

One Day
The Vennel is the site of the first kiss between Em and Dex, and the final poignant flashback of the 2024 series. The location was chosen as 'classic Edinburgh'. Netflix fan-site Tudum tells us that producers wanted 'a location that has the hustle and bustle of people… but also allows Em and Dex to appear static in the midst of it all'. On July 15 2024 a plaque appeared, announcing: 'It's one of the great cosmic mysteries. How someone can go from being a total stranger to the most important person in your life.' Another great cosmic mystery is whether this plaque has eloped with the Miss Jean Brodie Steps sign (see page 54).

The Prime of Miss Jean Brodie
In the 1969 film of Muriel Spark's novel, Miss Jean Brodie instructs her 'gels' to 'observe!' Edinburgh Castle from the top of the Vennel. Dewy-eyed, she tells them how Mary Queen of Scots lowered her baby down to the foot of the castle rock from one of these windows. Then her attention is drawn to a crushed McEwan's Export Ale box lying at their feet. 'Observe the litter!' she declaims, launching into a veneration of fascist dictator Mussolini and the tidiness of Italy's streets under his rule.

Rebus
Starring Richard Rankin, the 2024 BBC adaptation of Ian Rankin's Rebus novels features the Vennel Steps and has John Rebus living in Heriot Place with a view of the Telfer Wall from his window.

Johnny on the Run
The earliest film to feature the Vennel and Brown's Place was the 1953 adventure *Johnny on the Run*, directed by Lewis Gilbert. A young Polish refugee is taken in by his formidable Edinburgh aunt. Embroiled in a fight with local lads, he lets go of a pram with his baby cousin inside. After a nail-biting chase, he only just catches up with it as it teeters at the head of the Vennel Steps. The sequence is available on YouTube.

Memories & Trivia

Steps
There are 77 steps on the Vennel. In the 1960s it was paved with concrete blocks, then in the 1990s it was included in a major landscaping of the Grassmarket, and the steps replaced with Caithness stone.

Cattle
Engravings and early photographs show a contraption situated halfway up the Vennel, for measuring beasts on their way to the cattle market, where Edinburgh College of Art now stands. There were cattle pens at the back of tenements in Keir Street, at the top of the Vennel.

Noxious Trades
In the 19th century, so-called 'noxious trades' such as tanneries and tobacco factories clustered outside the city walls up to the back gardens of Brown's Place.

Bomb Shelters
During World War II there were two Anderson bomb shelters in Brown's Place. After the war, one was used to keep rabbits in and the other as a children's play hut.

Traditional Games
Popular games in the 1940s and '50s included peevers (hopscotch) chalked with pipe clay at the top of the Vennel, rounders on the drying greens, and henners (dares) on the railings beside the kindy (nursery).

Transportation
Daniel Brown, a tailor whose address is given as 'Vennel Walls, Edinburgh', was transported to Australia for life in January 1833. The following July, his wife Isabella was transported to Van Diemen's Land (Tasmania). Their crimes are not specified (www.oldscottish.com).

The Lovers Touch
Those puzzled by the 'Lovers Touch' plaque situated behind a fence on the right as you walk towards Heriot Place might seek clarification or further bamboozlement at www.kcymaerxthaere.com.

Bad Bairns
In the 1950s, youngsters sent a large wheel careering right down the Vennel. It bounced, narrowly missing residents the Salvation Army hostel sitting on the lower steps smoking clay pipes, then rolled over King's Stables Road landing near Granny's Green (recalled by Don Johnston, www.edinphoto.org.uk).

Image Credits

Page 14. Edinburgh Castle from the Grassmarket. Albumen print by George Washington Wilson (1823–93). Courtesy of Cornell University Library via Wikimedia Commons.

Page 16. Edinburgh Castle from the Vennel (1886). Engraving by Thomas H Shepherd.

Page 17. Ballantyne's Close. From James Grant's *Old and New Edinburgh* (c.1880).

Page 35. The Vennel and Old City Wall. Postcard.

Page 38. Bessie Watson, suffragette, aged nine. Courtesy of Edinburgh Libraries Capital Collections via Wikimedia Commons.

Page 41. Procession of suffragettes led by a woman in a tartan dress, a small girl (Bessie Watson) and three men in kilts, all playing bagpipes. Probably London, 1911. Courtesy of LSE Library via Flickr Commons.

Page 43. The Vennel in 1900. From *Edinburgh and Vicinity*, an album of photographs (nd) published by W R & S.

Page 52. William Burke as he appeared at the bar. Engraving made at the trial by George Lutenor. From *West Port Murders* (1829).

Page 54. Helen McDougal being chased by an Edinburgh mob on her release after her 'not proven' verdict. Engraving by Phiz (Hablot K Browne) from *The Chronicles of Crime; or, the New Newgate Calendar* (1891).

Page 57. Deacon Brodie with George Smith, one of his gang of burglars. Engraving by John Kay from *Kay's Portraits* (1837).

Page 60. Detail from a John Slezer print of Heriot's Hospital (now George Heriot's School). Originally this print appeared in *Theatrum Scotiae*; image reproduced from James Grant's *Old and New Edinburgh* (c.1880).

About the Contributors

ELSPETH WILLS is a researcher, interpreter and writer. She has written over a dozen books on subjects as varied as natural history, new town development and Scottish innovation. Most recently she co-authored with Martyn Routledge *Radicals Rebels & Royals PLC: A Pub Crawl through British History*. Elspeth lives in Brown's Place, on the Vennel.

JENNIE RENTON is a secondhand bookseller, copywriter and publishing freelancer. Her book reviews have appeared in the *Sunday Herald*. She was founder-editor of *Scottish Book Collector* magazine and edited *Folio* for the National Library of Scotland. She co-authored *Our Fathers Fought Franco* with Willy Maley, Lisa Croft and Tam Watters (Luath Press, 2023). Jennie lives in Keir Street, at the top of the Vennel.

ROGER EMMERSON is a retired architect and writer who also devotes his time to music and painting. His latest book, *Land of Stone: A journey through modern architecture in Scotland* was published by Luath Press in 2022.

The Vennel by Roger Emmerson (page 5) is available as an A4 or A3 poster. It can be ordered from www.mainpointbooks.co.uk.

Main Point BOOKS
Email: mainpointreads@gmail.com
Phone: 0131 228 4837
Website: www.mainpointbooks.co.uk
X: @mainpointbooks
Instagram: @mainpointbookshop

Local Organisations

GRASS & West Port Garden: www.grassmarketresidents.org

Brown's Place Residents' Association: www.bpra.org

Grassmarket Project: www.grassmarket.org

Lister Housing Cooperative: www.lister.coop

6VT: www.6vt.info

Dance Base: www.dancebase.co.uk

To donate to the upkeep of West Port Garden, please visit the West Port Community Garden page on GoFundMe or use the QR code below.